My
First
Book of
Nature

Mammals

Victoria Munson

WAYLAND

Editor: Victoria Brooker
Designer: Elaine Wilkinson

A cataloguing record for this title is
available at the British Library.

ISBN: 978 1 5263 0147 5

Printed in China

MIX
Paper from
responsible sources
FSC® C104740
FSC
www.fsc.org

Wayland, part of Hachette Children's
Group and published by Hodder
and Stoughton Limited.
www.hachette.co.uk

Acknowledgements:
All images and graphics: Shutterstock:
Cover: (main image) Eric Isselee: (tr)
oligo; (mr) Jirovo; (br) Erni; (tl)
Matthijs Wetterauw; (bl) Rudmer
Swerver; 1, 3b, 10 Leena Robinson; 2t,
21t KOO; 2b, 9 Martin Prochazkacz; 3,
12t, 12b Rudmer Zwerver; 4 Andrea
Izzotti; 5m Nigel Dowsett; 5b Ittai; 6
Mirko Graul; 7m Mikhail hoboton Popov;
7b juefraphoto; 8 Volodymyr Burdiak;
8m Mark Caunt; 10m Inge Jansen; 11
Pavel Krasensky;13 Erni; 14 Michael G.
Mill; 14b seawhisper; 15 scooperdigital;
16 Carl Mckie; 17t, 17b Erni; 18
Bildagentur Zoonar GmbH; 19t Erni; 19b
Guido Bissattini; 20 Dave Turner; 21b
LFRabanedo;

Contents

What is a Mammal?   4
Hedgehogs and Moles   6
Badgers and Foxes   8
Rabbits and Hares   10
Mice and Rats   12
Squirrels   14
Voles and Shrews   16
Stoats and Weasels   18
Deer   20
Follow that Footprint   22
Glossary and Index   24

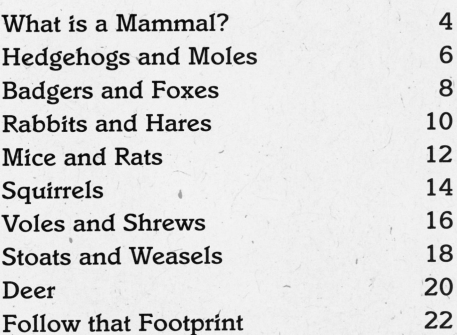

What is a Mammal?

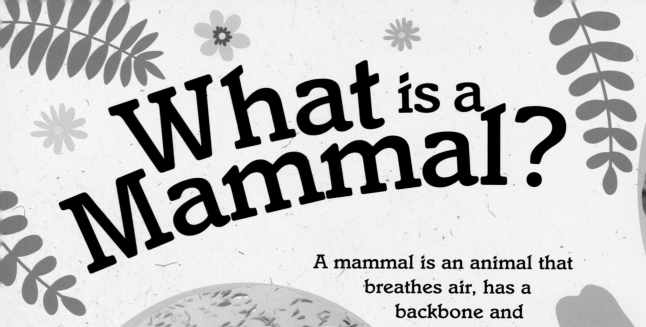

A mammal is an animal that breathes air, has a backbone and can produce milk to feed its young.

All mammals have hair at some stage in their life.

Some mammals, such as cows and horses, are active in the daytime.
Nocturnal animals, such as bats and badgers, are active at night.

British mammals live in many different habitats, such as woods, mountains and by rivers and the seashore.

Polar bears and penguins live at the cold poles.

Most mammals have teeth.

Mammals are found all over the world.

Camels and hyenas live in hot deserts.

Hedgehogs and Moles

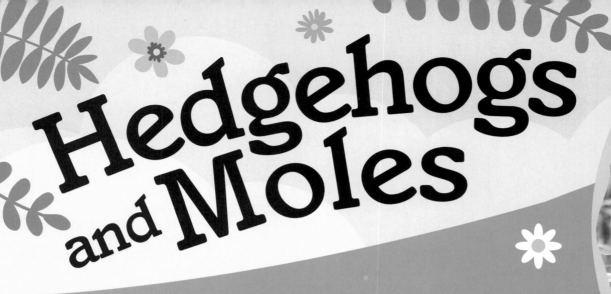

Hedgehogs have pointed spikes all over their bodies. An adult hedgehog has about 6,000 spikes.

When hedgehogs feel in danger, they roll themselves up into a spiky ball.

Hedgehogs are nocturnal, which means they sleep in the day and look for food at night.

In autumn, hedgehogs hibernate.

They dig a small hole and cover themselves with leaves.

When it is warmer in spring, they come out again.

Moles have black, velvety fur. They spend most of their lives underground.

Moles like to eat worms and insects.

Their strong, curved front paws are good for digging.

Badgers and Foxes

Badgers have a black and white striped face. They live in tunnels underground called setts. Badgers have sharp claws that help them to dig.

They sleep in the day and come out at night to feed.

Badgers are omnivores, which means they like to eat meat, such as worms or small animals, as well as plants such as fruits and roots.

Foxes have reddish-orange fur, with white bellies and a bushy tail.

Foxes live underground in dens.

A male fox is called a dog. A female fox is called a vixen. Young foxes are called cubs, pups or kits.

Foxes have large ears to help them hear mice or voles, which they love to eat.

Rabbits and Hares

Rabbits are brown with pointy ears and a white tail. They live in burrows underground. They eat grass and tree bark.

When frightened, rabbits will thump their back legs on the ground.

A male rabbit is called a buck. A female rabbit is called a doe.

Hares are bigger than rabbits and have much longer ears and legs. Hares live above ground.

Hares are the fastest land mammal in Britain.

Hares can run at 72kph.

Hares eat grass, berries and tree roots.

Young hares are called leverets.

Mice and Rats

Wood mice have golden-brown fur and large ears. They live in underground tunnels in fields, hedgerows or gardens.

Wood mice eat insects, grasses, berries and fungi.

Mice are good at climbing, jumping and swimming.

House mice have grey-brown fur and large ears. They live near humans, in tunnels under gardens or near houses.

House mice and rats will eat any old food that has been left lying around.

Rats have dark grey fur and a thick, scaly tail. Their tail helps them to balance.

Rats like to live in groups. A group of rats is called a mischief.

Squirrels

Grey squirrels have grey fur and a bushy tail that is as big as their body.

Red squirrels are reddish-brown, with a bushy tail and large tufted ears.

Squirrels don't hibernate, but they can sleep for days at a time.

Squirrels eat nuts and berries. In autumn, they bury the nuts and seeds so that they can eat them in the winter.

They use their long claws to open nutshells.

Squirrels' tails help them to balance as they jump from tree to tree.

15

Voles and Shrews

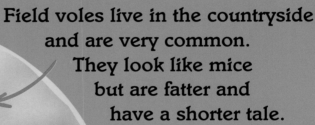

Field voles live in the countryside and are very common. They look like mice but are fatter and have a shorter tale.

Voles live in tunnels **underground.**

They eat plant roots and bulbs.

Water voles have dark brown fur, small ears and eyes, and a short tail.

Water voles are good swimmers.

Water shrews have dark grey fur that looks silvery when it is wet.

Voles and shrews don't live long lives because they have many predators, such as foxes, weasels and birds of prey.

Stoats and Weasels

Stoats have long, thin bodies. They have orangey-brown fur on their backs, white bellies and a black tip at the end of their tail.

Stoats are carnivores. This means they eat meat such as rabbits, birds and even foxes.

Young stoats and weasels are called kittens.

Weasels look like stoats but are a bit smaller. They don't have a black tip on their tale.

A group of stoats or weasels is called a caravan.

The weasel's slender body helps it to hunt voles and shrews in their burrows.

Stoats and weasels are very good at climbing.

19

Deer

Muntjac deer have reddish-brown fur. Male muntjacs have small antlers and tusks. Muntjacs are the smallest British deer.

Muntjac prefer to be on their own.

Muntjacs eat tree shoots and leaves, nuts and berries.

Red deer are the largest type of deer in Britain. Male deer have antlers, which are bony parts that grow on their head.

The antlers fall off in winter and grow back in spring.

Deer are herbivores, which means they eat only plants.

Follow that Footprint

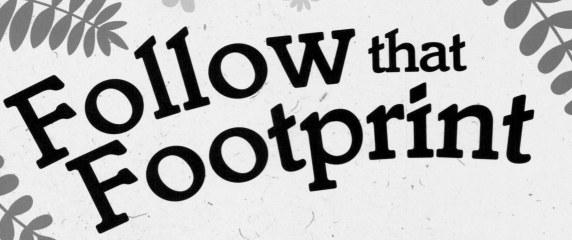

Sometimes it's hard to spot animals. Find out if a mammal has been nearby by looking for clues.

In soft mud, animals will leave footprints behind.

Deer

22

Look at the footprints and see if you can spot any in your local wildlife habitat.

Fox

Rabbit

Glossary and Index

carnivore an animal that eats mainly meat

habitat the natural environment in which an animal
or plant usually lives

herbivore an animal that eats only plants

hibernate to spend the winter sleeping

omnivore an animal that eats meat and plants

predator an animal that hunts, kills and eats other animals

badgers 4, 5
camels 5
deer 20, 21
foxes 8, 9
hares 10, 11
hedgehogs 6, 7

mice 12, 13
moles 6, 7
nocturnal animals 4
penguins 5
polar bears 5
rabbits 10, 11

rats 13
shrews 17
stoats 18, 19
squirrels 14, 15
voles 16
weasels 18, 19

Birds
9781526301208

What is a Bird?
Garden Birds
City Birds
Woodland Birds
Ducks, Swans and Geese
Birds of Prey
Owls
Farmland Birds
Follow that Footprint
Glossary and Index

Flowers
9781526301499

What are flowers?
Garden flowers
Park flowers
Seashore flowers
Mountain flowers
Water flowers
Meadow flowers
Heathland flowers
Woodland flowers
Flower life cycle
Glossary and index

Mammals
9781526301475

What is a Mammal?
Hedgehogs and Moles
Badgers and Foxes
Rabbits and Hares
Mice and Rats
Squirrels
Voles and Shrews
Stoats and Weasels
Deer
Follow that Footprint
Glossary and Index

Minibeasts
9781526301512

What are minibeasts?
Beetles
Bugs
Butterflies
Wasps and Bees
Seaside minibeasts
Millipedes, Centipedes
    and Woodlice
Slugs, snails and spiders
Ants, worms and earwigs
Where to find minibeasts
Glossary and index

Seashore
9781526301536

What is the seashore?
Rock pool creatures
Seaweed
Shells
Birds
Insects
Fish
Mammals
Plants
Seashore shells
Glossary and index

Trees
9781526301550

What is a tree?
Oaks
Willows
Silver birch, Alder, Hazel
Sycamore, Field Maple,
    London Plane
Lime, Rowan, Whitebeam
Chestnuts and Beech
Yew, Monkey Puzzle, Juniper
Scots Pine, Norway Spruce,
    Douglas Fir
Leaves and seeds
Glossary and index

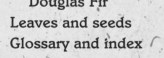